Mindfulness
Day
by Day

Blue Mountain Arts®

New and Best-Selling Titles

By Susan Polis Schutz:
To My Daughter with Love on the Important Things in Life
To My Grandchild with Love
To My Son with Love

By Douglas Pagels:
Always Remember How Special You Are to Me
Required Reading for All Teenagers
The Next Chapter of Your Life
You Are One Amazing Lady

By Marci:
Angels Are Everywhere!
Friends Are Forever
10 Simple Things to Remember
To My Daughter
To My Granddaughter
To My Mother
To My Son
You Are My "Once in a Lifetime"

By Wally Amos, with Stu Glauberman:
The Path to Success Is Paved with Positive Thinking

By Minx Boren:
Friendship Is a Journey
Healing Is a Journey

By Carol Wiseman:
Emerging from the Heartache of Loss

Anthologies:
A Daybook of Positive Thinking
A Son Is Life's Greatest Gift
Dream Big, Stay Positive, and Believe in Yourself
Girlfriends Are the Best Friends of All
God Is Always Watching Over You
The Love Between a Mother and Daughter Is Forever
Nothing Fills the Heart with Joy like a Grandson
There Is Nothing Sweeter in Life Than a Granddaughter
There Is So Much to Love About You… Daughter
Think Positive Thoughts Every Day
Words Every Woman Should Remember
You Are Stronger Than You Know

Mindfulness Day by Day

How to Create Peace and Happiness in Your Daily Life

A Blue Mountain Arts® Collection
Edited by Patricia Wayant

Blue Mountain Press™
Boulder, Colorado

Library of Congress Control Number: 2016957085
ISBN: 978-1-68088-117-2

◪ and Blue Mountain Press are registered in U.S. Patent and Trademark Office.
Certain trademarks are used under license.

Printed in China.
First Printing: 2017

Blue Mountain Arts, Inc.
P.O. Box 4549, Boulder, Colorado 80306

Contents

Practice Mindfulness
Every Day

Don't just have minutes in the day; have moments in time. Balance out any bad with the good you can provide. Know that you are capable of amazing results. Surprise yourself by discovering new strength inside.

Add a meaningful page to the diary of each day. Do things no one else would even dream of. There is no greater gift than the kind of inner beauty you possess. Do the things you do... with love.

Walk along the pathways that enrich your happiness. Taking care of the "little things" is a big necessity. Don't be afraid of testing your courage. Life is short, but it's long enough to have excitement and serenity.

Don't let the important things go unsaid. Do the things that brighten your life and help you on your way. Live to the fullest; make each day count.

— Collin McCarty

Live in the Moment

To be in the moment means
to sit in reflection, in silence,
allowing for thoughts and emotions
to flow freely.
It means to take a breather
from your everyday schedule
to enjoy the simple things in life.

To be in the moment means
not letting life pass you by.
It allows you to experience
each moment for what it is
and then let it go
like a feather floating in the wind.

To be in the moment allows us
to see the many blessings we have —
the wonderful gifts
that we so quickly look past
in our day-to-day lives.
It means truly and entirely living.

— Lamisha Serf-Walls

Today, make time in your busy schedule to contemplate and slow way down... to gaze at the landscape and marvel at the beauty and majesty of the trees. Look up until you can almost touch that big, out-of-reach blue sky. Focus on being thankful that you can see and take in all this magnificent splendor.

Listen to the sounds around you. Hear the birds speaking their own language and imagine them talking to you. Let yourself hear the traffic noise expressing its collective cadence of the universe. Be still and tune into the melodies in your heart for inspiration; let yourself appreciate that you can also make your own music and sing your own song.

Breathe in and appreciate the life-giving air. Breathe out and don't worry about anything except being where you are now. Comprehend and value the harmony of your relationship with every living thing. Be thankful for the people who are positive influences in your life.

Take the time to fall in love with life.

— Donna Fargo

Focus on the Life
You've Been Given

Embrace every moment you are given. Cherish the people, places, and things that fill your life with so much warmth and joy. Take time when others around you are rushing, and feel intensely when it would be easier not to feel at all. Understand that things go wrong, mistakes get made, and bad stuff happens, but choose to focus on the beauty and goodness in the world. Recognize that each new day is a gift that will never come again.

— Anna Marie Edwards

If you look to others for fulfillment,
you will never truly be fulfilled.
If your happiness depends on money,
you will never be happy with yourself.
Be content with what you have;
rejoice in the way things are.
When you realize there is nothing lacking,
the whole world belongs to you.

— Lao Tzu

The real voyage of discovery consists not in seeking
out new landscapes but in having new eyes.

— Marcel Proust

A Simple Lesson
in Mindfulness

This is a very short and simple lesson in mindfulness, a way in which we can bring peace to ourselves in any moment. Practicing this twenty minutes each day, preferably in the morning, will change your life.

Sit comfortably, with your back as straight as possible. Let your entire body relax. Close your eyes very gently. Bring your full awareness to your breath as you breathe in and out through your nose. You can say to yourself: "I am breathing in. I am breathing out. In. Out." Or: "I am breathing in peace. I am breathing out tension. Peace. Tension."

Simply notice whatever takes you from your breathing — a thought, sound, itch, daydream — and acknowledge it by naming it. Then, very gently, without judgment, go back to your breathing.

By practicing this twenty minutes in the morning, every day, you will learn how powerful your breath is, and you will become more and more aware that you can turn to your breath at any time during the day to bring peace to your heart.

— Ruth Fishel

Here's the thing... life changes a lot.
So cherish the things you love most,
and keep a sharp eye out
for the good in everyday life.
Be aware of pitfalls —
those situations that don't feel quite right —
and keep peace in your heart.

Even when it's raining,
when the world around you
is spinning and flailing,
when the door won't open
and the car won't start —
keep peace in your heart.

— Ashley Rice

In the degree that we are filled with this Spirit
of Peace by thus opening ourselves to its inflow
does it pour through us, so that we carry it with us
wherever we go. In the degree that we thus open
ourselves do we become magnets to attract peace
from all sources; and in the degree that we attract
and embody it in ourselves are we able to give it
forth to others.

— Ralph Waldo Trine

Peace: it does not mean to be in a place
where there is no noise, trouble, or hard
work. It means to be in the midst of those
things and still be calm in your heart.

— Author Unknown

Master Your
Own Mind

When you say to yourself, "I am going to have a pleasant visit or a pleasant journey," you are literally sending elements and forces ahead of your body that will arrange things to make your visit or journey pleasant. When before the visit or the journey or the shopping trip you are in a bad humor, or fearful or apprehensive of something unpleasant, you are sending unseen agencies ahead of you, which will make some kind of unpleasantness. Our thoughts, or in other words, our state of mind, is ever at work "fixing up" things good or bad in advance.

— Prentice Mulford

The universe is change; our life is what our thoughts make it.

— Marcus Aurelius

Your living is determined not so much by what life brings to you as by the attitude you bring to life; not so much by what happens to you as by the way your mind looks at what happens.

Circumstances and situations do color life, but you have been given the mind to choose what the color will be.

— John Homer Miller

The Root of Happiness

If we want to know what happiness is, we must seek it, not as if it were a pot of gold at the end of the rainbow, but among human beings who are living richly and fully the good life. If you observe a really happy man, you will find him building a boat, writing a symphony, educating his children, growing double dahlias in his garden. He will not be searching for happiness... he will have become aware that he is happy in the course of living twenty-four crowded hours in the day.

— W. Beran Wolfe

Happiness cannot come from without. It must come from within. It is not what we see and touch or that which others do for us which makes us happy; it is that which we think and feel and do, first for the other fellow and then for ourselves.

— Helen Keller

Happiness is a butterfly, which when pursued, is always just beyond your grasp, but which, if you sit down quietly, may light upon you.

— Nathaniel Hawthorne

Look for Joy
in Simple Things

When you arise in the morning, think
of what a precious privilege it is to be
alive — to breathe, to think, to enjoy,
to love.

— Marcus Aurelius

To find the air and the water exhilarating; to
be refreshed by a morning walk or an evening
saunter... to be thrilled by the stars at night;
to be elated over a bird's nest or a wildflower
in spring — these are some of the rewards of
the simple life.

— John Burroughs

Live to the fullest, and make each day count. Don't let the important things go unsaid. Have simple pleasures in this complex world. Be a joyous spirit and a sensitive soul. Take those long walks that would love to be taken. Explore those sunlit paths that would love to oblige. Don't just have minutes in the day; have moments in time.

— Douglas Pagels

Each morning we are born again.
What we do today is what
matters most.
— Buddha

Be intent upon the perfection
of the present day.

— William Law

Life Begins Each Morning!

Life is a day — this day. All past days are gone beyond reviving. All days that still may come for you or me are veiled in the great mystery, and for all we know, there may not be another for either of us. Therefore this day is Life, and life begins anew with it....

The greatest fact in life is this, that it never is too late to start again. History overflows with startling examples of this truth. And if we had access to the vast number of unrecorded lives, we would find an overwhelming mass of supporting testimony.

However discouraging your days may have been thus far, keep this thought burning brightly in your mind — Life Begins Each Morning!

— Leigh Mitchell Hodges

Begin doing what you want to do now.
We are not living in eternity. We have only
this moment, sparkling like a star in our
hand — and melting like a snowflake.

— Francis Bacon

Begin at once to live, and count each separate
day as a separate life.

— Seneca

Look to this day,
for it is life —
the very life of life.
In its brief course lie all
the verities and realities of your existence:
the bliss of growth, the glory of action,
the splendor of beauty.
For yesterday is already a dream
and tomorrow is only a vision;
but today, well lived,
makes every yesterday a dream of happiness
and every tomorrow a vision of hope.
Look well, therefore, to this day!

— Ancient Sanskrit Poem

Release Old Habits

The simile of a path is convenient to illustrate the theory of the mind regarding habits. A certain sort of vibration is set in motion, starting in one particular area and ending in another. The next time it starts, the same beginning and end mark its course. The same vibration happens again and again, and with each additional characteristic of a path we have one that may be applied to a habit: a well-worn path becomes a rut, and whatever travels along the margin is bound to slip into the depression.

— Nathan Oppenheim, MD

Cultivate only the habits that you are willing should master you.

— Elbert Hubbard

The mind is slow in unlearning what it has been long in learning.

— Seneca

Be Fully Present

The days of our lives fly by like the wind,
as if we were swiftly gliding down
a mysterious highway.
We no sooner pass a major landmark
than it seems to vanish
in the rearview mirror.
But sometimes we need
to take stock and reflect,
to pull over, smell the roses,
and see the starlight...
to celebrate everything we have been,
everything we are,
and everything we will be.

— Michael Shevlane

Always hold fast to the present.
Every situation, indeed every moment,
is of infinite value, for it is the
representative of a whole eternity.

— Johann Wolfgang von Goethe

Find Your Center

Flow with whatever is happening and let your mind be free. Stay centered by accepting whatever you are doing. This is the ultimate.

— Chuang Tzu

Let go of your mind and then be mindful. Close your ears and listen!

— Rumi

When I dance I dance; when I sleep I sleep; yes, when I walk alone in a beautiful orchard, if my thoughts have been concerned with extraneous incidents for some part of the time, for some other part I lead them back again to the walk, to the orchard, to the sweetness of solitude, and to myself.

— Michel de Montaigne

Learn to be silent. Let your quiet mind listen and absorb.

— Pythagoras

Master Stillness

We all have within us a center of stillness surrounded by silence.

— Dag Hammarskjöld

To the mind that is still, the whole universe surrenders.

— Lao Tzu

To return to your original state of being,
You must become a master of stillness.
Activity for health's sake,
Never carried to the point of strain,
Must alternate with perfect stillness.
Sitting motionless as a rock,
Turn next to stillness of mind.
Close the gates of the senses.
Fix your mind upon one object or,
Even better, enter a state
Of objectless awareness.
Turn the mind in upon itself
And contemplate the inner radiance.

— Author Unknown

The Testing

To walk when others are running,
To whisper when others are shouting;
To sleep when others are restless,
To smile when others are angry;
To work when others are idle,
To pause when others are hurrying;
To pray when others are doubting,
To think when others are in confusion;
To face turmoil, yet feel composure;
To know inner calm in spite of
    everything —
This is the test of serenity.

— Doris Lacasse

Life is a series of natural and spontaneous changes. Don't resist them — that only creates sorrow. Let reality be reality. Let things flow naturally forward in whatever way they like.

— Lao Tzu

Every day, be full of awareness of the beauty around you.

— Barbara Cage

Master Acceptance

Acceptance means that you
can find the serenity within
to let go of the past
with its mistakes and regrets,
move into the future
with a new perspective,
and appreciate the opportunity
to take a second chance.

Acceptance means that when
difficult times come into your life,
you'll find security again and comfort
to relieve any pain.
You'll find new dreams, fresh hopes,
and forgiveness of the heart.

Acceptance does not mean
that you will always be perfect.
It simply means that
you'll always overcome imperfection.

Acceptance is the road to peace —
　　letting go of the worst,
holding on to the best,
　　and finding the hope inside
that continues throughout life.

Acceptance is the heart's best defense,
　　love's greatest asset,
and the easiest way to keep believing
　　in yourself and others.
— Regina Hill

Say "Yes" to Life

Enthusiasm for life will bring a radiance to your face and voice. People are attracted by the contagious joy that fills you with laughter, that inspires you and those you touch to greater achievement of your own true potential.

Say "Yes" to beauty; the beauty of sunrise and sunset; of star-filled sky and the wonder of its endlessness; the beauty of flowers, of a child's smile; the beauty of poetry, prose, and music. There is so much beauty all around you; take time to see it, hear it, smell it, and be comforted by it! The world isn't drab — appreciate its marvelous colors, sounds, and fragrances.

Say "Yes" to opportunity. Regardless of financial conditions, the unemployment situation, age or education, there are greater opportunities today than ever in the world's history. It takes alertness to recognize opportunity, work to qualify, and courage to embrace it. Never hesitate because you haven't done the work before, or think you don't measure up. You are far, far greater than you have demonstrated. Say "I can" and go on to the greater unfoldment of your mind and spirit.

Say "Yes" to the immense good in life and you will find so great a blessing that there shall not be room enough to receive it.

— Paul K. Poulsen

Live in a Spirit of Love

Love illumines the mind, gives new life to every fiber in your being, removes almost every burden, and eases the whole path of existence. Love removes entirely all anger, hatred, revenge, ill will, and similar states — a matter of great importance, for no one can live an ideal life while such states of mind remain.... The person who loves everybody with that larger loving kindness has taken a long step upward into that life that is real life. This is not mere sentiment, but the expression of an exact scientific fact. A strong, continuous love will bring all good to anyone who lives and acts as he inwardly feels.

— Christian D. Larson

Fill your heart with the kindness of friends, the caring of everyone you love, and the richness of memories you wouldn't trade for anything.

— Douglas Pagels

You will find as you look back upon your life that the moments that stand out, the moments when you have really lived, are the moments when you have done things in a spirit of love.

— Henry Drummond

Gentle Words
of Encouragement

As you reach forward with one hand, accept the advice of those who have gone before you, and in the same manner reach back with the other hand to those who follow you; for life is a fragile chain of experiences held together by love. Take pride in being a strong link in that chain. Discipline yourself, but do not be harsh. The pleasures of life are yours to be taken. Share them with others, but always remember that you, too, have earned the right to partake.

Know those who love you; love is the finest of all gifts and is received only to be given. Embrace those who truly love you, for they are few in a lifetime. Then return that love tenfold, radiating it from your heart to fill their lives as sunlight warms the darkest corners of the earth. Love is a journey, not a destination; travel its path daily. Do this and your troubles will be as fleeting as footprints in the sand. When loneliness is your companion and all about you seems to be gone, pause and listen, for the sound of loneliness is silence, and in silence we hear best. Listen well, and your moments of silence will always be broken by the gentle words of encouragement spoken by those who love you.

— Tim Murtaugh

Keep Kindness
in Your Heart

Three things in human life are important. The first is to be kind. The second is to be kind. And the third is to be kind.

— Henry James

Kindness is the inability to remain at ease in the presence of another person who is ill at ease, the inability to remain comfortable in the presence of another who is uncomfortable, the inability to have peace of mind when one's neighbor is troubled.

— Samuel H. Holdenson

Go beyond yourself and reach out to other people with a sincere love, respect, caring, and understanding of their needs.

— Susan Polis Schutz

Master Forgiveness

Forgiveness is letting go of the pain
and accepting what has happened,
because it will not change.

Forgiveness is dismissing the blame.
Choices were made that caused the hurt;
we each could have chosen differently,
but we didn't.

Forgiveness is looking at the pain,
learning the lessons it has produced,
and understanding
what we have learned.

Forgiveness allows us to move on
toward a better understanding
of universal love
and our true purpose.

Forgiveness is knowing that love
is the answer to all questions,
and that we all
are in some way connected.

Forgiveness is starting over
with the knowledge
that we have gained.
I forgive you, and I forgive myself.
I hope you can do the same.

— Judith Mammay

This, Too, Shall Pass

When some great sorrow, like a mighty river,
  Flows through your life with peace-destroying power,
And dearest things are swept from sight forever,
  Say to your heart each trying hour:
  "This, too, shall pass away."

When ceaseless toil has hushed your song of gladness,
  And you have grown almost too tired to pray,
Let this truth banish from your heart its sadness,
  And ease the burdens of each trying day:
    "This, too, shall pass away."

When fortune smiles, and, full of mirth and pleasure,
  The days are flitting by without a care,
Lest you should rest with only earthly treasure,
  Let these few words their fullest import bear:
    "This, too, shall pass away."

When earnest labor brings you fame and glory,
  And all earth's noblest ones upon you smile,
Remember that life's longest, grandest story
  Fills but a moment in earth's little while:
    "This, too, shall pass away."

— Ella Wheeler Wilcox

Look Within

It is in your power to withdraw into yourself whenever you desire. Perfect tranquility within consists in the good ordering of the mind — the realm of your own.

— Marcus Aurelius

Remember when life's path is steep to keep your mind even.

— Horace

Within you is your very own universe.
A bit of stardust is blowing your way —
a bit of light and a bit of wonder.
Follow your leanings;
listen to the whispers of your soul.

— Linda E. Knight

Learn to retreat within the Silence, and
listen to the voice of your soul — it will tell
you many great things.

— Yogi Ramacharaka

Open Yourself
to All That Is Beautiful

Never lose an opportunity of seeing anything that is beautiful; for beauty is God's handwriting — a wayside sacrament. Welcome it in every fair face, in every fair sky, in every fair flower, and thank God for it as a cup of blessing.

— Ralph Waldo Emerson

The longer I live the more my mind dwells upon the beauty and wonder of the world.... I have loved the feel of the grass under my feet, and the sound of the running streams by my side. The hum of the wind in the treetops has always been good music to me, and the face of the fields has often comforted me more than the faces of men.

I am in love with this world.... I have tilled its soil, I have gathered its harvest, I have waited upon its seasons, and always have I reaped what I have sown.... I have climbed its mountains, roamed its forests, sailed its waters, crossed its deserts, felt the sting of its frosts, the oppression of its heats, the drench of its rains, the fury of its winds, and always have beauty and joy waited upon my goings and comings.

— John Burroughs

We need to feel more
to understand others
We need to love more
to be loved back
We need to cry more
to cleanse ourselves
We need to laugh more
to enjoy ourselves

We need to be honest and fair
when interacting with people
We need to establish a strong ethical basis
as a way of life
We need to see more
than our own fantasies
We need to hear more
and listen to the needs of others

We need to give more
and take less
We need to share more
and own less
We need to realize the importance
    of the family
as a backbone to stability
We need to look more
and realize that we are not so
    different from one another

We need to create a world where
we can trust one another
We need to create a world where
we can all peacefully live
the life we choose

— Susan Polis Schutz

Spend Time in Nature

I would have all busy people make times in their lives... when they should try to be alone with nature and their own hearts. They should try to realize the quiet, unwearying life that manifests itself in field and wood. They should wander alone in solitary places where the hazel-hidden stream makes music and the bird sings out of the heart of the forest; in meadows where the flowers grow brightly... I will go further and say that a man who does not wish to do these things is shutting one of the doors of his spirit, a door through which many sweet and true things come in.

— Arthur C. Benson

Nature is not separate from me; she is mine alike with my body; and in moments of true life, I feel my identity with her.

— Amos Bronson Alcott

Stoop and touch the earth, and receive its influence; touch the flower, and feel its life; face the wind, and have its meaning; let the sunlight fall on the open hand as if you could hold it. Something may be grasped from them all, invisible yet strong. It is the sense of a wider existence — wider and higher.

— Richard Jefferies

Meld with the Earth
Meditation

This uncomplicated yet incredibly refreshing exercise works best if you are somewhat removed from the sounds of traffic and people — in a forest, a country field, a secluded yard, or a quiet park.

Lie on your back, either on top of a blanket or on the bare ground, and make yourself comfortable. Close your eyes and take a few deep breaths. Continue breathing steadily. Begin to relax each part of your body, beginning with your toes. Then move up through every single part of your body and consciously relax each part as you go: your ankles, calves, knees, thighs, buttocks, hips, stomach, spine, chest, shoulders, arms, elbows, fingers, neck, chin, mouth, nose, eyes, forehead, and scalp. Once every part of your body is relaxed, feel your body become heavy and sink into the earth. Allow the earth to support your weight completely.

Begin listening to the sounds around you — birds chirping, a squirrel twittering, the stillness in the air, or maybe water flowing. Take a deep breath and notice any smells — cut grass, dirt, leaves, flowers. Become aware of the ground beneath you. Open your eyes and take in whatever is above you — treetops, sky, clouds. Lie there and enjoy for as long as you would like, knowing you are a part of it all.

Practice Gratitude

Gratitude consists of being more aware
of what you have than what you don't.

— Author Unknown

If we knew how much the habit of being thankful might do
for us, I am sure we would take time out every day to count
up a few of our blessings. When the spirit of thankfulness
takes its place in our consciousness, we radiate life from the
very center of our being to the world about us.

— Author Unknown

Be thankful that you don't already have
    everything you desire.
If you did, what would there be to look forward to?
Be thankful when you don't know something,
for it gives you the opportunity to learn.
Be thankful for the difficult times.
During those times, you grow.
Be thankful for your limitations,
because they give you opportunities for improvement.
Be thankful for each new challenge,
because it will build your strength and character.
Be thankful for your mistakes.
They will teach you valuable lessons.
Be thankful when you're tired and weary,
because it means you've made an effort.
It's easy to be thankful for the good things.
A life of rich fulfillment comes to those who
    are also thankful for the setbacks.
Gratitude can turn a negative into a positive.
Find a way to be thankful for your troubles,
and they can become your blessings.

— Author Unknown

There Is So Much to Be Thankful For

We don't often
take the time out of our busy lives
to think about all
the beautiful things
and to be thankful for them
If we did reflect on these things
we would realize how very
lucky and fortunate we really are

I am very thankful
for the love of my husband —
which is so complete and fulfilling
and is based on honesty, equality
intellectualism and romance

I am very thankful
for the love of my children —
which is all encompassing
and is based on teaching, tenderness
sensitivity, caring and hugging

I am very thankful
that I am able to love
and that the love is returned to me

I am very thankful
that I am healthy
and that the people I love are healthy

I am very thankful
that I have dreams to follow
and goals to strive for

I am very thankful
for the beauty of nature —
magnificent mountains
the colorful leaves
the smell of the flowers
the roaring of the waves
the setting sun
the rising moon

Everywhere I look
I see the wonders of nature
and I feel so proud
to be a small part of it

I am very thankful
for all the good people in the world
I am very thankful
that I have good friends

I am very thankful
to be alive
in a time when
we can make the world
a better place
to live in

— Susan Polis Schutz

Life Is Not a Race

Never be in a hurry; do everything quietly and in a calm spirit. Do not lose your inward peace for anything whatsoever, even if your whole world seems upset.

— Francis de Sales

Rest is not idleness, and to lie sometimes on the grass under trees on a summer's day, listening to the murmur of the water or watching the clouds float across the sky, is by no means a waste of time.

— Sir J. Lubbock

Don't run through life so fast that you forget not only where you've been but also where you're going. Life is not a race but a journey to be savored each step of the way.

— Nancye Sims

Take a Deep Breath

There's a good reason people always advise "take a deep breath" when you're upset or nervous. Deep breathing is calming. It releases tension. Because you have to think about doing it, deep breathing forces you to focus on the moment.

For centuries, practitioners of yoga have known how deep breathing can immediately improve the way you feel. Besides helping to relax the body, yogic breathing infuses your blood with oxygen, boosting your energy.

Try the following exercise:

- Find a quiet spot where you can sit comfortably in a chair or cross-legged on the floor.
- Close your eyes and visualize a leaf falling from a tree into a slow-moving creek.
- Still visualizing the leaf, let your breath in and out slowly and peacefully. Inhale deeply and exhale through your nose.
- Repeat twenty times, then gradually let your breath return to normal.
- Finally, take a few moments to sit with your eyes closed and notice the difference in how you feel.

Be Truly Alone

Settle into yourself
Be truly alone

And not the kind of alone
that makes your heart sore
but the kind that causes
your breath to slow
your limbs to go weightless
your thoughts to fall from you
one by one

Embrace the moment
that leaves you in
complete solitude
Welcome these times
as a gift of peace
for your spirit and soul

Your sustenance
— Elle Mastro

Remember that being alone
doesn't always mean being lonely;
it can be a beautiful experience
of finding your creativity,
your heartfelt feelings,
and the calm and quiet peace
    deep inside you.

— Jacqueline Schiff

Be Mindful
While Eating

The life of man is formed from the things he eats.
Prepare simple meals, chew well, and sup lightly.

— Leonardo da Vinci

The spirit cannot endure the body when overfed,
but, if underfed, the body cannot endure the spirit.

— Francis de Sales

When walking, walk.
When eating, eat.

— Zen Proverb

- Eat only when you are hungry.
- Place your food on a plate — do not be tempted to eat out of a box.
- Dine while sitting at a table.
- Eliminate distractions, such as the TV or reading materials.
- Observe the arrangement of food on your plate — notice the colors, textures, and smells.
- Think about what it took to produce your meal — where did the foods come from?
- Try to taste each individual ingredient.
- Do not hurry; eat slowly.
- Take small bites and chew thoroughly before swallowing.
- Notice when you are full and then stop eating.
- Sit quietly when you are done.
- How does your body feel?

Be Mindful
in Your Relationships

In our busy lives, we often forget that there is more than just bills to pay, phone calls to return, and errands to run. There are people in our lives who need to be hugged, who need to be loved. There are people in our lives who need their accomplishments noticed and praised. We need to remember that a heart is like a garden that needs to be tended to and nourished with what only another heart can give — love and appreciation, devotion and honesty.

— Tracia Gloudemans

Each day is an opportunity to share our hearts, our love, and our lives to the fullest. Sometimes that means just making the most out of the smallest things — like listening to each other, holding each other's hand, or just being together.

— Star Nakamoto

When you talk to those who matter most, open the door to your heart. The wider it is, the easier it will be for things like compassion and understanding to come inside. And it just naturally follows... the more wonderful visitors you have, the more your life will shine.

— Douglas Pagels

Be Mindful
in Your Work

Choose to do the things that will reflect well... on your ability, your integrity, your spirit, your health, your tomorrows, your smiles, your dreams, and yourself.

— Douglas Pagels

You are not here merely to make a living. You are here in order to enable the world to live more amply, with greater vision, with a finer spirit of hope and achievement. You are here to enrich the world.

— Woodrow T. Wilson

Few persons realize how much of their happiness is dependent upon their work, upon the fact that they are kept busy and not left to feed upon themselves. Happiness comes most to persons who seek her least, and think least about her. It is not an object to be sought; it is a state to be induced. It must follow and not lead. It must overtake you, and not you overtake it.

— John Burroughs

If you want to be healthy morally, mentally, and physically, just let go. Let go of the little annoyances of everyday life, the irritations and the petty vexations that cross your path daily. Don't take them up, nurse them, pet them, and brood over them. They are not worthwhile. Let them go!

— Author Unknown

I love my past. I love my present. I'm not ashamed of what I've had, and I'm not sad because I have it no longer.

— Colette

Let go...
  of guilt; it's okay to make
  the same mistakes again.
Let go...
  of obsessions; they seldom
  turn out the way you planned.
Let go...
  of hate; it's a waste of love.
Let go...
  of blaming others; you are
  responsible for your own destiny.
Let go...
  of fear; it's a waste of faith.
Let go...
  of despair; change comes from
  acceptance and forgiveness.
Let go...
  of the past; the future is
  here — right now.

— Kathleen O'Brien

Fill Your Mind with Positive Thoughts

Our own worst enemy cannot harm us as much as our unwise thoughts. No one can help us as much as our own compassionate thoughts.

— Buddha

There is only one way to happiness and that is to cease worrying about things which are beyond the power of our will.

— Epictetus

We cannot choose how many years we will live, but we can choose how much life those years will have. We cannot control the beauty of our face, but we can control the expression on it. We cannot control life's difficult moments, but we can choose to make life less difficult. We cannot control the negative atmosphere of the world, but we can control the atmosphere of our minds. Too often we try to choose and control things we cannot. Too seldom we choose to control what we can... our attitude.

— Author Unknown

Take Nothing for Granted

Take nothing for granted: the sheer act
of waking each day; fresh air upon your cheek;
each effort expended on self or another —
walking the dog, shopping for food,
toiling at home, in an office, or on the road.
Every moment is rare, short, and full of glory.
Every word is magic;
a story achieved through will.
Marvel at nature's moods as mirror of your own.
Recall a sunrise or sunset,
a flock of geese in the sky.
Care about parents or children as fragile gifts
like a petal on a rose, like a song from one bird.
Praise the simple or complex —
the invention of flight above clouds;
the wheel; the bathtub; a rocking chair.

We rise and fall in the moon or a wave,
in a smile or many tears.
And being brave is to be alive
as we give and share love always,
only and ever to survive.

— Rochelle Lynn Holt

Desiderata

Go placidly amid the noise and the haste, and remember what peace there may be in silence. ↵ As far as possible, without surrender, be on good terms with all persons. Speak your truth quietly and clearly; and listen to others, even to the dull and ignorant; they too have their story. ↵ Avoid loud and aggressive persons; they are vexatious to the spirit. ↵ If you compare yourself with others, you may become vain or bitter, for always there will be greater and lesser persons than yourself. ↵ Enjoy your achievements as well as your plans. Keep interested in your own career, however humble; it is a real possession in the changing fortunes of time. ↵ Exercise caution in your business affairs, for the world is full of trickery. But let this not blind you to what virtue there is; many persons strive for high ideals, and everywhere life is full of heroism. ↵

Be yourself. Especially, do not feign affection. Neither be cynical about love; for in the face of all aridity and disenchantment, it is as perennial as the grass. ⟵ Take kindly the counsel of the years, gracefully surrendering the things of youth. Nurture strength of spirit to shield you in sudden misfortune. But do not distress yourself with dark imaginings. Many fears are born of fatigue and loneliness. ⟵ Beyond a wholesome discipline, be gentle with yourself. ⟵ You are a child of the universe no less than the trees and the stars; you have a right to be here. ⟵ And whether or not it is clear to you, no doubt the universe is unfolding as it should. Therefore be at peace with God, whatever you conceive Him to be. ⟵ And whatever your labors and aspirations, in the noisy confusion of life, keep peace in your soul. ⟵ With all its sham, drudgery and broken dreams, it is still a beautiful world. Be cheerful. Strive to be happy. ⟵

— Max Ehrmann

Respond with Serenity

There is no need to give up your serenity for the sake of getting something accomplished. In fact, accomplishment comes more surely when your efforts are calm and your spirit is peaceful.

Consider how very much more you can get done when your energy is not being sapped away by a frenzied mind. True serenity is not the absence of action, but rather action with integrity, confidence, and a steadfastness of purpose.

The world may very well be swirling around you in a constant turmoil. But you don't have to adopt that turmoil as your own.

The more frenzied and hurried life becomes, the more serene and unperturbed you have the opportunity to be. Whatever you can accomplish in a hectic and chaotic state, you can accomplish much more powerfully with peaceful, calm determination.

When you're confronted with turmoil, respond with serenity. It will lift you to a higher level of experience and accomplishment.

— Ralph S. Marston, Jr.

Life's Most
Important Treasures

Joy
   in your heart,
   your mind,
   your soul.
Happiness
   with yourself
   and with the world.
Harmony.
Courage
   to feel, to need,
   to reach out.
Freedom
   to let yourself
   be bound by love.
Friendship.

Wisdom
   to learn, to change,
   to let go.
Acceptance
   of the truth
   and beauty within yourself.
Growth.
Pleasure
   in all that you see
   and touch
   and do.
Peace
   with yourself
   and with the universe.

— Maureen Doan

Day by Day...

ay you find serenity and tranquility in a world you may
not always understand. May you discover enough goodness
in others to believe in a world of peace. May a kind word,
a reassuring touch, and a warm smile be yours every day
of your life, and may you give these gifts as well as receive
them. Remember the sunshine when the storm seems
unending. Teach love to those who know hate, and let that
love embrace you as you go into the world.

May the teachings of those you admire become part of you, so that you may call upon them. Remember, those whose lives you have touched and who have touched yours are always a part of you, even if the encounters were less than you would have wished. It is the content of the encounter that is more important than its form. May you not become too concerned with material matters, but instead place immeasurable value on the goodness in your heart. Find time in each day to see beauty and love in the world around you. Realize that each person has limitless abilities, but each of us is different in our own way. What you may feel you lack in one regard may be more than compensated for in another. Learn to view everything as a worthwhile experience. May you find enough inner strength to determine your own worth by yourself and not be dependent on another's judgment of your accomplishments. May you always feel loved.

— Sandra Sturtz Hauss

ACKNOWLEDGMENTS

We gratefully acknowledge the permission granted by the following authors, publishers, and authors' representatives to reprint poems or excerpts in this publication:

Susan Polis Schutz for "Go beyond yourself…" and "There Is So Much to Be Thankful For." Copyright © 1990, 1992 by Stephen Schutz and Susan Polis Schutz. And for "We need to feel more…." Copyright © 1972 by Continental Publications. Renewed © 2000 by Stephen Schutz and Susan Polis Schutz. All rights reserved.

Lamisha Serf-Walls for "Live in the Moment." Copyright © 2017 by Lamisha Serf-Walls. All rights reserved.

PrimaDonna Entertainment Corp. for "Today, make time in your…" by Donna Fargo. Copyright © 2013 by PrimaDonna Entertainment Corp. All rights reserved.

Sterling Publishing Co., Inc., for "This is a very short and simple…" from PEACE IN OUR HEARTS, PEACE IN THE WORLD by Ruth Fishel. Copyright © 2008 by Ruth Fishel. All rights reserved.

Rochelle Lynn Holt for "Take Nothing for Granted." Copyright © 2017 by Rochelle Lynn Holt. All rights reserved.

Ralph S. Marston, Jr., for "Respond with Serenity." Copyright © 2003 by Ralph S. Marston, Jr. Used by permission. Originally published in "The Daily Motivator" at www.greatday.com. All rights reserved.

A careful effort has been made to trace the ownership of selections used in this anthology in order to obtain permission to reprint copyrighted material and give proper credit to the copyright owners. If any error or omission has occurred, it is completely inadvertent, and we would like to make corrections in future editions provided that written notification is made to the publisher:

BLUE MOUNTAIN ARTS, INC., P.O. Box 4549, Boulder, Colorado 80306.